GOD'S OWN WORD TO THOSE WHO ARE MISTREATED

Compiled by Pastor Scott Markle

Shepherding the Flock Ministries

7971 Washington St. ❖ Melvin, MI 48454
(810) 378-5323
www.shepherdingtheflock.com

God's Own Word: To Those Who Are Mistreated
Compiled by Pastor Scott Markle

Printed in the United States of America

ISBN 9780615902685

Shepherding the Flock Ministries
7971 Washington St.
Melvin, MI 48454
(810) 378-5323
www.shepherdingtheflock.com

CONTENTS

INTRODUCTION

The "God's Own Word" booklet series is intended to reveal only God's own Word on a particular matter. Each booklet provides a compilation of Biblical passages on a particular subject and categorizes those passages under a set of headings related to that subject. In addition, portions of each passage are highlighted in bold italics in order to point out the parts of the passage that are the most relevant to the subject. In this manner, the reader is instructed *by God's own Word.* I pray that these booklets may spiritually edify, exhort, and encourage your heart.

For the Excellency of the Knowledge of Christ Jesus our Lord, Abiding in Christ, and Christ in us,
Pastor Scott Markle

Do Good to Those Who Mistreat You

Matthew 5:38-48 - Ye have heard that it hath been said, An eye for an eye, and a tooth for a tooth: *but I say unto you, That ye resist not evil: but whosoever shall smite thee on thy right cheek, turn to him the other also.* And if any man will sue thee at the law, and take away thy coat, let him have thy cloke also. And whosoever shall compel thee to go a mile, go with him twain. Give to him that asketh thee, and from him that would borrow of thee turn not thou away. Ye have heard that it hath been said, Thou shalt love thy neighbour, and hate thine enemy. *But I say unto you, Love your enemies, bless them that curse you, do good to them that hate you, and pray for them which despitefully use you, and persecute you; that ye may be the children of your Father which is in heaven*: for he maketh his sun to rise on the evil and on the good, and sendeth rain on the just and on the unjust. For if ye love them which love you, what reward have ye? Do not even the publicans the same? And if ye salute your brethren only, what do ye more than others? Do not even the publicans so? *Be ye therefore perfect, even as your Father which is in heaven is perfect.*

Luke 6:27-36 - *But I say unto you which hear, Love your enemies, do good to them which hate you, bless them that curse you, and pray for them which despite-fully use you. And unto him that smiteth thee on the one cheek offer also the other*; and him that taketh away thy cloke forbid not to take thy coat also. Give to every man that asketh of thee; *and of him that taketh away thy goods ask them not again.* And as ye would that men should do to you, do ye also to them likewise. For if ye love them which love you, what thank have ye? For sinners also love those that love them. And if ye do good to them which do good to you, what thank have ye? For sinners also do even the same. And if ye lend to them of whom ye hope to receive, what thank have ye? For sinners also lend to sinners, to receive as much again. *But love ye your enemies, and do good, and lend, hoping for nothing again; and your reward shall be great, and ye shall be the children of the Highest: for he is kind unto the unthankful and to the evil. Be ye therefore merciful, as your Father also is merciful.*

Romans 12:14, 17-21 - *Bless them which persecute you: bless, and curse not* . . . . *Recompense to no man evil for evil.* Provide things honest in the sight of all men. *If it be possible, as much as lieth in you, live peaceably with all men.* Dearly beloved, avenge not yourselves, but rather give place unto wrath: for it is written, Vengeance is mine; I will repay, saith the Lord. *Therefore if thine enemy hunger, feed him; if he thirst, give him drink: for in so doing thou shalt heap coals of fire on his head. Be not overcome of evil, but over-come evil with good.*

Proverbs 25:21-22 - *If thine enemy be hungry, give him bread to eat; and if he be thirsty, give him water to* *drink*: for thou shalt heap coals of fire upon his head, *and the LORD shall reward thee*.

1 Thessalonians 5:15 - *See that none render evil for evil unto any man; but ever follow that which is good*, both among yourselves, and to all men.

1 Peter 3:9-12 - *Not rendering evil for evil, or railing for railing: but contrariwise blessing*; knowing that ye are thereunto called, that ye should inherit a blessing. *For he that will love life, and see good days, let him refrain his tongue from evil, and his lips that they speak no guile: let him eschew evil, and do good; let him seek peace, and ensue it. For the eyes of the Lord are over the righteous, and his ears are open unto their prayers: but the face of the Lord is against them that do evil.*

Exodus 23:4-5 - If thou meet *thine enemy's* ox or his ass going astray, *thou shalt surely bring it back to him again*. If thou see the ass *of him that hateth thee* lying under his burden, *and wouldest forbear to help him, thou shalt surely help with him*.

Psalm 35:12-15 - They rewarded me evil for good to the spoiling of my soul. *But as for me, when they were sick, my clothing was sackcloth: I humbled my soul with fasting; and my prayer returned into mine own bosom. I behaved myself as though he had been my friend or brother: I bowed down heavily, as one that mourneth for his mother.* But in mine adversity they rejoiced, and gathered themselves together: yea, the abjects gathered themselves together against me, and I knew it not; they did tear me, and ceased not.

Proverbs 24:17-18 - *Rejoice not when thine enemy falleth, and let not thine heart be glad when he stumbleth: lest the LORD see it, and it displease him, and he turn away his wrath from him.*

James 5:9 - *Grudge not one against another, brethren, lest ye be condemned: behold, the judge standeth before the door.*

Psalm 7:3-5 - O LORD my God, if I have done this; *if there be iniquity in my hands; if I have rewarded evil unto him that was at peace with me; (yea, I have delivered him that without cause is mine enemy:) let the enemy persecute my soul, and take it; yea, let him tread down my life upon the earth*, and lay mine honour in the dust. Selah.

Proverbs 17:13 - *Whoso rewardeth evil for good, evil shall not depart from his house.*

Ezekiel 25:15-17 - Thus saith the Lord GOD; *Because the Philistines have dealt by revenge, and have taken vengeance with a despiteful heart*, to destroy it for the old hatred; *therefore thus saith the Lord GOD; Behold, I will stretch out mine hand upon the Philistines*, and I will cut off the Cherethims, and destroy the remnant of the sea coast. *And I will execute great vengeance upon them with furious rebukes; and they shall know that I am the LORD, when I shall lay my vengeance upon them.*

Luke 9:52-56 - And sent messengers before his face: and they went, and entered into a village of the Samaritans, to make ready for him. *And they did not receive him*, because his face was as though he would go to

Jerusalem. *And when his disciples James and John saw this, they said, Lord, wilt thou that we command fire to come down from heaven, and consume them*, even as Elias did? *But he turned, and rebuked them, and said, Ye know not what manner of spirit ye are of. For the Son of man is not come to destroy men's lives, but to save them.* And they went to another village.

Love Your Enemies

Matthew 5:43-44 - Ye have heard that it hath been said, Thou shalt love thy neighbour, and hate thine enemy. *But I say unto you, Love your enemies, bless them that curse you, do good to them that hate you, and pray for them which despitefully use you, and persecute you.*

Luke 6:27-28, 32, 35 - *But I say unto you which hear, Love your enemies*, do good to them which hate you, bless them that curse you, and pray for them which despitefully use you . . . . *For if ye love them which love you, what thank have ye? For sinners also love those that love them* . . . . *But love ye your enemies*, and do good, and lend, hoping for nothing again; *and your reward shall be great, and ye shall be the children of the Highest*: for he is kind unto the unthankful and to the evil.

1 Corinthians 13:4-7 - *Charity suffereth long, and is kind; charity envieth not; charity vaunteth not itself, is not puffed up, doth not behave itself unseemly, seeketh not her own, is not easily provoked, thinketh no evil; rejoiceth not in iniquity, but rejoiceth in the truth; beareth all things, believeth all things, hopeth all things, endureth all things.*

Proverbs 10:12 - *Hatred stirreth up strifes: but love covereth all sins.*

Proverbs 17:9 - *He that covereth a transgression seeketh love; but he that repeateth a matter separateth very friends.*

Song of Solomon 8:7 - *Many waters cannot quench love, neither can the floods drown it*: if a man would give all the substance of his house for love, it would utterly be contemned.

Ephesians 5:1-2 - Be ye therefore followers of God, as dear children; *and walk in love, as Christ also hath loved us, and hath given himself for us an offering and a sacrifice to God for a sweetsmelling savour.*

Romans 5:6-8 - For when we were yet without strength, *in due time Christ died for the ungodly.* For scarcely for a righteous man will one die: yet peradventure for a good man some would even dare to die. *But God commendeth his love toward us, in that, while we were yet sinners, Christ died for us.*

Colossians 3:14 - *And above all these things put on charity, which is the bond of perfectness.*

Romans 12:9-10 - *Let love be without dissimulation. Abhor that which is evil; cleave to that which is good. Be kindly affectioned one to another with brotherly love; in honour preferring one another.*

1 Peter 1:22 - Seeing ye have purified your souls in obeying the truth through the Spirit unto unfeigned love of the brethren, *see that ye love one another with a pure heart fervently.*

1 Peter 4:8 - *And above all things have fervent charity among yourselves: for charity shall cover the multitude of sins.*

1 John 2:9-11 - *He that saith he is in the light, and hateth his brother, is in darkness even until now. He that loveth his brother abideth in the light, and there is none occasion of stumbling in him. But he that hateth his brother is in darkness, and walketh in darkness, and knoweth not whither he goeth, because that darkness hath blinded his eyes.*

1 John 3:10-18 - In this the children of God are manifest, and the children of the devil: whosoever doeth not righteousness is not of God, neither he that loveth not his brother. *For this is the message that ye heard from the beginning, that we should love one another. Not as Cain, who was of that wicked one, and slew his brother.* And wherefore slew he him? Because his own works were evil, and his brother's righteous. Marvel not, my brethren, if the world hate you. *We know that we have passed from death unto life, because we love the brethren. He that loveth not his brother abideth in death. Whosoever hateth his brother is a murderer: and ye know that no murderer hath eternal life abiding in him. Hereby perceive we the love of God, because he laid down his life for us: and we ought to lay down our lives for the brethren. But whoso hath this world's good, and seeth his brother have need, and shutteth up his bowels of compassion from him, how dwelleth the love of God in him? My little children, let us not love in word, neither in tongue; but in deed and in truth.*

Maintain a Tender Heart and A Forgiving Spirit

Matthew 5:7 - *Blessed are the merciful: for they shall obtain mercy.*

Luke 6:35-37 - But love ye your enemies, and do good, and lend, hoping for nothing again; and your reward shall be great, and ye shall be the children of the Highest: for he is kind unto the unthankful and to the evil. *Be ye therefore merciful, as your Father also is merci-ful. Judge not, and ye shall not be judged: condemn not, and ye shall not be condemned: forgive, and ye shall be forgiven.*

Matthew 6:9-15 - After this manner therefore pray ye: Our Father which art in heaven, hallowed be thy name. Thy kingdom come. Thy will be done in earth, as it is in heaven. Give us this day our daily bread. *And forgive us our debts, as we forgive our debtors.* And lead us not into temptation, but deliver us from evil: for thine is the kingdom, and the power, and the glory, for ever. Amen. *For if ye forgive men their trespasses, your heavenly Father will also forgive you: but if ye forgive not men their trespasses, neither will your Father forgive your trespasses.*

Mark 11:25-26 - And when ye stand praying, forgive, if ye have ought against any: that your Father also which is in heaven may forgive you your trespasses. But if ye do not forgive, neither will your Father which is in heaven forgive your trespasses.

Luke 17:3-4 - Take heed to yourselves: If thy brother trespass against thee, rebuke him; *and if he repent, forgive him. And if he trespass against thee seven times in a day, and seven times in a day turn again to thee, saying, I repent; thou shalt forgive him.*

Matthew 18:15, 21-35 - *Moreover if thy brother shall trespass against thee, go and tell him his fault between thee and him alone: if he shall hear thee, thou hast gained thy brother* . . . . Then came Peter to him, and said, *Lord, how oft shall my brother sin against me, and I forgive him? Till seven times? Jesus saith unto him, I say not unto thee, Until seven times: but, Until seventy times seven.* Therefore is the kingdom of heaven likened unto a certain king, which would take account of his servants. *And when he had begun to reckon, one was brought unto him, which owed him ten thousand talents. But forasmuch as he had not to pay, his lord commanded him to be sold, and his wife, and children, and all that he had, and payment to be made.* The servant therefore fell down, and worshipped him, saying, Lord, have patience with me, and I will pay thee all. *Then the lord of that servant was moved with compassion, and loosed him, and forgave him the debt. But the same servant went out, and found one of his fellowservants, which owed him an hundred pence*: and he laid hands on him, and took him by the throat, saying, Pay me that thou owest. And his fellowservant fell down at his feet, and besought him, saying, Have patience with me, and I will pay thee all. ***And he would not: but went and cast him into prison, till he should pay the debt.*** So when his fellowservants saw what was done, they were very sorry, and came and told unto their lord all that was done. ***Then his lord, after that he had called him, said unto him, O thou wicked servant, I forgave thee all that debt, because thou desiredst me: shouldest not thou also have had compassion on thy fellowservant, even as I had pity on thee? And his lord was wroth, and delivered him to the tormentors, till he should pay all that was due unto him. So likewise shall my heavenly Father do also unto you, if ye from your hearts forgive not every one his brother their trespasses.***

Ephesians 4:29-32 - Let no corrupt communication proceed out of your mouth, but that which is good to the use of edifying, that it may minister grace unto the hearers. And grieve not the holy Spirit of God, whereby ye are sealed unto the day of redemption. ***Let all bitterness, and wrath, and anger, and clamour, and evil speaking, be put away from you, with all malice: and be ye kind one to another, tenderhearted, forgiving one another, even as God for Christ's sake hath forgiven you.***

Colossians 3:12-13 - ***Put on therefore, as the elect of God, holy and beloved, bowels of mercies, kindness, humbleness of mind, meekness, longsuffering; forbearing one another, and forgiving one another, if any man have a quarrel against any: even as Christ forgave you, so also do ye.***

Proverbs 14:21-22 - ***He that despiseth his neighbour sinneth***: but he that hath mercy on the poor, happy is he. ***Do they not err that devise evil? But mercy and truth shall be to them that devise good.***

Hebrews 12:15 - *Looking diligently lest any man fail of the grace of God; lest any root of bitterness springing up trouble you, and thereby many be defiled.*

James 3:14-18 - *But if ye have bitter envying and strife in your hearts, glory not, and lie not against the truth. This wisdom descendeth not from above, but is earthly, sensual, devilish.* For where envying and strife is, there is confusion and every evil work. *But the wisdom that is from above is first pure, then peaceable, gentle, and easy to be intreated, full of mercy and good fruits, without partiality, and without hypocrisy. And the fruit of righteousness is sown in peace of them that make peace.*

Ephesians 4:1-3 - I therefore, the prisoner of the Lord, beseech you that ye walk worthy of the vocation wherewith ye are called, *with all lowliness and meekness, with longsuffering, forbearing one another in love; endeavouring to keep the unity of the Spirit in the bond of peace.*

Luke 23:34 - *Then said Jesus, Father, forgive them; for they know not what they do.* And they parted his raiment, and cast lots.

Acts 7:57-60 - *Then they cried out with a loud voice, and stopped their ears, and ran upon him with one accord, and cast him out of the city, and stoned him*: and the witnesses laid down their clothes at a young man's feet, whose name was Saul. *And they stoned Stephen*, calling upon God, and saying, Lord Jesus, receive my spirit. *And he kneeled down, and cried with a loud voice, Lord, lay not this sin to their charge.* And when he had said this, he fell asleep.

Rejoice When You Suffer
For Christ's Sake

1 Peter 3:14 - *But and if ye suffer for righteousness' sake, happy are ye: and be not afraid of their terror, neither be troubled.*

1 Peter 4:12-16 - *Beloved, think it not strange concerning the fiery trial which is to try you, as though some strange thing happened unto you: but rejoice, inasmuch as ye are partakers of Christ's sufferings; that, when his glory shall be revealed, ye may be glad also with exceeding joy. If ye be reproached for the name of Christ, happy are ye; for the spirit of glory and of God resteth upon you*: on their part he is evil spoken of, but on your part he is glorified. But let none of you suffer as a murderer, or as a thief, or as an evildoer, or as a busybody in other men's matters. *Yet if any man suffer as a Christian, let him not be ashamed; but let him glorify God on this behalf.*

Luke 6:22-23 - *Blessed are ye, when men shall hate you, and when they shall separate you from their company, and shall reproach you, and cast out your name as evil, for the Son of man's sake. Rejoice ye in that day, and leap for joy: for, behold, your reward is great in heaven*: for in the like manner did their fathers unto the prophets.

Matthew 5:10-12 - *Blessed are they which are perse-cuted for righteousness' sake: for theirs is the kingdom of heaven. Blessed are ye, when men shall revile you, and persecute you, and shall say all manner of evil against you falsely, for my sake. Rejoice, and be exceeding glad: for great is your reward in heaven*: for so persecuted they the prophets which were before you.

2 Corinthians 12:9-10 - And he said unto me, My grace is sufficient for thee: for my strength is made perfect in weakness. *Most gladly therefore will I rather glory in my infirmities, that the power of Christ may rest upon me. Therefore I take pleasure in infirmities, in re-proaches, in necessities, in persecutions, in distresses for Christ's sake: for when I am weak, then am I strong.*

Wait with Patience Upon the Lord's Deliverance

Proverbs 20:22 - *Say not thou, I will recompense evil; but wait on the LORD, and he shall save thee.*

James 5:6-11 - Ye [rich men] *have condemned and killed the just*; and he [the just] doth not resist you. *Be patient therefore, brethren, unto the coming of the Lord.* Behold, the husbandman waiteth for the precious fruit of the earth, and hath long patience for it, until he receive the early and latter rain. *Be ye also patient; stablish your hearts: for the coming of the Lord draweth nigh.* Grudge not one against another, brethren, lest ye be condemned: behold, the judge standeth before the door. *Take, my brethren, the prophets*, who have spoken in the name of the Lord, *for an example of suffering affliction, and of patience. Behold, we count them happy which endure. Ye have heard of the patience of Job, and have seen the end of the Lord; that the Lord is very pitiful, and of tender mercy.*

Hebrews 12:3 - *For consider him* [our Lord Jesus Christ] *that endured such contradiction of sinners against himself, lest ye be wearied and faint in your minds.*

1 Peter 2:19-23 - *For this is thankworthy, if a man for conscience toward God endure grief, suffering wrongfully.* For what glory is it, if, when ye be buffeted for your faults, ye shall take it patiently? *But if, when ye do well, and suffer for it, ye take it patiently, this is acceptable with God. For even hereunto were ye called: because Christ also suffered for us, leaving us an example, that ye should follow his steps*: who did no sin, neither was guile found in his mouth: *who, when he was reviled, reviled not again; when he suffered, he threatened not; but committed himself to him that judgeth righteously*.

1 Peter 3:14-18 - *But and if ye suffer for righteousness' sake, happy are ye: and be not afraid of their terror, neither be troubled; but sanctify the Lord God in your hearts: and be ready always to give an answer to every man that asketh you a reason of the hope that is in you with meekness and fear: having a good conscience*; that, whereas they speak evil of you, as of evildoers, they may be ashamed that falsely accuse your good conversation in Christ. *For it is better, if the will of God be so, that ye suffer for well doing, than for evil doing. For Christ also hath once suffered for sins, the just for the unjust*, that he might bring us to God, being put to death in the flesh, but quickened by the Spirit.

2 Corinthians 12:9-10 - *And he said unto me, My grace is sufficient for thee: for my strength is made perfect in weakness.* Most gladly therefore will I rather glory in my infirmities, *that the power of Christ may rest upon me*. Therefore I take pleasure in infirmities, in reproaches, in necessities, in persecutions, in distresses for Christ's sake: *for when I am weak, then am I strong*.

Deuteronomy 32:43 - *Rejoice, O ye nations, with his people*: for he will avenge the blood of his servants, and will render vengeance to his adversaries, *and will be merciful unto his land, and to his people*.

Psalm 3:1-8 - LORD, how are they increased that trouble me! Many are they that rise up against me. *Many there be which say of my soul, There is no help for him in God. Selah. But thou, O LORD, art a shield for me; my glory, and the lifter up of mine head. I cried unto the LORD with my voice, and he heard me out of his holy hill. Selah. I laid me down and slept; I awaked; for the LORD sustained me. I will not be afraid of ten thousands of people, that have set themselves against me round about.* Arise, O LORD; save me, O my God: for thou hast smitten all mine enemies upon the cheek bone; thou hast broken the teeth of the ungodly. *Salvation belongeth unto the LORD: thy blessing is upon thy people.* Selah.

Psalm 5:7-12 - *But as for me, I will come into thy house in the multitude of thy mercy: and in thy fear will I worship toward thy holy temple. Lead me, O LORD, in thy righteousness because of mine enemies; make thy way straight before my face.* For there is no faithfulness in their mouth; their inward part is very wickedness; their throat is an open sepulchre; they flatter with their tongue. Destroy thou them, O God; let them fall by their own counsels; cast them out in the multitude of their transgressions; for they have rebelled against thee. *But let all those that put their trust in thee rejoice: let them ever shout for joy, because thou defendest them: let them also that love thy name be joyful in thee. For thou, LORD, wilt bless the righteous; with favour wilt thou compass him as with a shield.*

Psalm 7:1-2, 9-10 - *O LORD my God, in thee do I put my trust: save me from all them that persecute me, and deliver me*: lest he tear my soul like a lion, rending it in pieces, while there is none to deliver . . . . *Oh let the wickedness of the wicked come to an end; but establish the just*: for the righteous God trieth the hearts and reins. *My defence is of God, which saveth the upright in heart.*

Psalm 9:1-16 - *I will praise thee, O LORD, with my whole heart; I will shew forth all thy marvellous works. I will be glad and rejoice in thee: I will sing praise to thy name, O thou most High.* When mine enemies are turned back, they shall fall and perish at thy presence. *For thou hast maintained my right and my cause; thou satest in the throne judging right.* Thou hast rebuked the heathen, thou hast destroyed the wicked, thou hast put out their name for ever and ever. O thou enemy, destructions are come to a perpetual end: and thou hast destroyed cities; their memorial is perished with them. *But the LORD shall endure for ever: he hath prepared his throne for judgment. And he shall judge the world in righteousness, he shall minister judgment to the people in uprightness. The LORD also will be a refuge for the oppressed, a refuge in times of trouble. And they that know thy name will put their trust in thee: for thou, LORD, hast not forsaken them that seek thee. Sing praises to the LORD, which dwelleth in Zion: declare among the people his doings.* When he maketh inquisition for blood, he remembereth them: *he forgetteth not the cry of the humble. Have mercy upon me, O LORD; consider my trouble which I suffer of them that hate me, thou that liftest me up from the gates of death: that I may shew forth all thy praise in the gates of the daughter of Zion: I will rejoice in thy salvation.*

The heathen are sunk down in the pit that they made: in the net which they hid is their own foot taken. *The* *LORD is known by the judgment which he executeth*: the wicked is snared in the work of his own hands. Higgaion. Selah.

Psalm 10:12-18 - *Arise, O LORD; O God, lift up thine* *hand: forget not the humble.* Wherefore doth the wicked contemn God? He hath said in his heart, Thou wilt not require it. Thou hast seen it; for thou beholdest mischief and spite, to requite it with thy hand: *the poor* *committeth himself unto thee; thou art the helper of* *the fatherless*. Break thou the arm of the wicked and the evil man: seek out his wickedness till thou find none. *The LORD is King for ever and ever*: the heathen are perished out of his land. *LORD, thou hast heard the de-* *sire of the humble: thou wilt prepare their heart, thou* *wilt cause thine ear to hear: to judge the fatherless and* *the oppressed, that the man of the earth may no more* *oppress.*

Psalm 11:1-2, 7 - *In the LORD put I my trust*: how say ye to my soul, Flee as a bird to your mountain? For, lo, the wicked bend their bow, they make ready their arrow upon the string, that they may privily shoot at the up-right in heart . . . . *For the righteous LORD loveth* *righteousness; his countenance doth behold the* *upright.*

Psalm 12:5 - *For the oppression of the poor, for the* *sighing of the needy, now will I arise, saith the LORD; I* *will set him in safety from him that puffeth at him.*

Psalm 13:1-6 - How long wilt thou forget me, O LORD? For ever? How long wilt thou hide thy face from me?

How long shall I take counsel in my soul, having sorrow in my heart daily? How long shall mine enemy be exalted over me? ***Consider and hear me, O LORD my God***: lighten mine eyes, lest I sleep the sleep of death; lest mine enemy say, I have prevailed against him; and those that trouble me rejoice when I am moved. ***But I have trusted in thy mercy; my heart shall rejoice in thy salvation. I will sing unto the LORD, because he hath dealt bountifully with me.***

Psalm 17:6-12 - *I have called upon thee, for thou wilt hear me, O God: incline thine ear unto me, and hear my speech. Shew thy marvellous lovingkindness, O thou that savest by thy right hand them which put their trust in thee from those that rise up against them. Keep me as the apple of the eye, hide me under the shadow of thy wings, from the wicked that oppress me, from my deadly enemies, who compass me about.* They are inclosed in their own fat: with their mouth they speak proudly. They have now compassed us in our steps: they have set their eyes bowing down to the earth; like as a lion that is greedy of his prey, and as it were a young lion lurking in secret places.

Psalm 18:1-6, 16-24, 46-49 - *I will love thee, O LORD, my strength. The LORD is my rock, and my fortress, and my deliverer; my God, my strength, in whom I will trust; my buckler, and the horn of my salvation, and my high tower. I will call upon the LORD, who is worthy to be praised: so shall I be saved from mine enemies.* The sorrows of death compassed me, and the floods of ungodly men made me afraid. The sorrows of hell compassed me about: the snares of death prevented me. *In my distress I called upon the LORD, and cried unto my God: he heard my voice out of his temple, and* *my cry came before him, even into his ears* . . . . *He sent from above, he took me, he drew me out of many waters. He delivered me from my strong enemy, and from them which hated me: for they were too strong for me.* They prevented me in the day of my calamity: *but the LORD was my stay. He brought me forth also into a large place; he delivered me, because he delighted in me.* The LORD rewarded me according to my righteousness; according to the cleanness of my hands hath he recompensed me. *For I have kept the ways of the LORD, and have not wickedly departed from my God. For all his judgments were before me, and I did not put away his statutes from me. I was also upright before him, and I kept myself from mine iniquity.* Therefore hath the LORD recompensed me according to my righteousness, according to the cleanness of my hands in his eyesight . . . . *The LORD liveth; and blessed be my rock; and let the God of my salvation be exalted.* It is God that avengeth me, and subdueth the people under me. *He delivereth me from mine enemies: yea, thou liftest me up above those that rise up against me: thou hast delivered me from the violent man. Therefore will I give thanks unto thee, O LORD, among the heathen, and sing praises unto thy name.*

Psalm 22:11-24 - *Be not far from me; for trouble is near; for there is none to help.* Many bulls have compassed me: strong bulls of Bashan have beset me round. They gaped upon me with their mouths, as a ravening and a roaring lion. I am poured out like water, and all my bones are out of joint: my heart is like wax; it is melted in the midst of my bowels. My strength is dried up like a potsherd; and my tongue cleaveth to my jaws; and thou hast brought me into the dust of death. For dogs have compassed me: the assembly of the wicked have inclosed me: they pierced my hands and my feet. I may tell all my bones: they look and stare upon me. They part my garments among them, and cast lots upon my vesture. *But be not thou far from me, O LORD: O my strength, haste thee to help me. Deliver my soul from the sword; my darling from the power of the dog. Save me from the lion's mouth: for thou hast heard me from the horns of the unicorns. I will declare thy name unto my brethren: in the midst of the congregation will I praise thee.* Ye that fear the LORD, praise him; all ye the seed of Jacob, glorify him; and fear him, all ye the seed of Israel. *For he hath not despised nor abhorred the affliction of the afflicted; neither hath he hid his face from him; but when he cried unto him, he heard.*

Psalm 23:5 - *Thou preparest a table before me in the presence of mine enemies: thou anointest my head with oil; my cup runneth over.*

Psalm 25:1-3, 15-21 - *Unto thee, O LORD, do I lift up my soul. O my God, I trust in thee*: let me not be ashamed, let not mine enemies triumph over me. Yea, let none that wait on thee be ashamed: let them be ashamed which transgress without cause . . . . *Mine eyes are ever toward the LORD; for he shall pluck my feet out of the net. Turn thee unto me, and have mercy upon me; for I am desolate and afflicted. The troubles of my heart are enlarged: O bring thou me out of my distresses. Look upon mine affliction and my pain; and forgive all my sins.* Consider mine enemies; for they are many; and they hate me with cruel hatred. *O keep my soul, and deliver me: let me not be ashamed; for I put my trust in thee. Let integrity and uprightness preserve me; for I wait on thee.*

Psalm 27:1-14 - *The LORD is my light and my salvation; whom shall I fear? The LORD is the strength of my life; of whom shall I be afraid?* When the wicked, even mine enemies and my foes, came upon me to eat up my flesh, they stumbled and fell. *Though an host should encamp against me, my heart shall not fear: though war should rise against me, in this will I be confident. One thing have I desired of the LORD, that will I seek after; that I may dwell in the house of the LORD all the days of my life, to behold the beauty of the LORD, and to enquire in his temple. For in the time of trouble he shall hide me in his pavilion: in the secret of his tabernacle shall he hide me; he shall set me up upon a rock. And now shall mine head be lifted up above mine enemies round about me: therefore will I offer in his tabernacle sacrifices of joy; I will sing, yea, I will sing praises unto the LORD. Hear, O LORD, when I cry with my voice: have mercy also upon me, and answer me. When thou saidst, Seek ye my face; my heart said unto thee, Thy face, LORD, will I seek. Hide not thy face far from me; put not thy servant away in anger: thou hast been my help; leave me not, neither forsake me, O God of my salvation. When my father and my mother forsake me, then the LORD will take me up. Teach me thy way, O LORD, and lead me in a plain path, because of mine enemies. Deliver me not over unto the will of mine enemies*: for false witnesses are risen up against me, and such as breathe out cruelty. *I had fainted, unless I had believed to see the goodness of the LORD in the land of the living. Wait on the LORD: be of good courage, and he shall strengthen thine heart: wait, I say, on the LORD.*

Psalm 31:1-24 - *In thee, O LORD, do I put my trust; let me never be ashamed: deliver me in thy righteousness. Bow down thine ear to me; deliver me speedily: be thou my strong rock, for an house of defence to save me. For thou art my rock and my fortress; therefore for thy name's sake lead me, and guide me. Pull me out of the net that they have laid privily for me: for thou art my strength. Into thine hand I commit my spirit: thou hast redeemed me, O LORD God of truth.* I have hated them that regard lying vanities: *but I trust in the LORD. I will be glad and rejoice in thy mercy: for thou hast considered my trouble; thou hast known my soul in adversities; and hast not shut me up into the hand of the enemy: thou hast set my feet in a large room. Have mercy upon me, O LORD, for I am in trouble: mine eye is consumed with grief, yea, my soul and my belly.* For my life is spent with grief, and my years with sighing: my strength faileth because of mine iniquity, and my bones are consumed. I was a reproach among all mine enemies, but especially among my neighbours, and a fear to mine acquaintance: they that did see me without fled from me. I am forgotten as a dead man out of mind: I am like a broken vessel. For I have heard the slander of many: fear was on every side: while they took counsel together against me, they devised to take away my life. *But I trusted in thee, O LORD: I said, Thou art my God. My times are in thy hand: deliver me from the hand of mine enemies, and from them that persecute me. Make thy face to shine upon thy servant: save me for thy mercies' sake. Let me not be ashamed, O LORD; for I have called upon thee*: let the wicked be ashamed, and let them be silent in the grave. Let the lying lips be put to silence; which speak grievous things proudly and contemptuously against the righteous. *Oh how great is thy goodness, which thou hast laid up for them that fear* *thee; which thou hast wrought for them that trust in thee before the sons of men! Thou shalt hide them in the secret of thy presence from the pride of man: thou shalt keep them secretly in a pavilion from the strife of tongues. Blessed be the LORD: for he hath shewed me his marvellous kindness in a strong city. For I said in my haste, I am cut off from before thine eyes: nevertheless thou heardest the voice of my supplications when I cried unto thee. O love the LORD, all ye his saints: for the LORD preserveth the faithful*, and plentifully rewardeth the proud doer. *Be of good courage, and he shall strengthen your heart, all ye that hope in the LORD.*

Psalm 35:1-3, 9-12, 17-28 - *Plead my cause, O LORD, with them that strive with me: fight against them that fight against me. Take hold of shield and buckler, and stand up for mine help. Draw out also the spear, and stop the way against them that persecute me: say unto my soul, I am thy salvation . . . . And my soul shall be joyful in the LORD: it shall rejoice in his salvation. All my bones shall say, LORD, who is like unto thee, which deliverest the poor from him that is too strong for him, yea, the poor and the needy from him that spoileth him?* False witnesses did rise up; they laid to my charge things that I knew not. They rewarded me evil for good to the spoiling of my soul . . . . Lord, how long wilt thou look on? *Rescue my soul from their destructions, my darling from the lions. I will give thee thanks in the great congregation: I will praise thee among much people.* Let not them that are mine enemies wrongfully rejoice over me: neither let them wink with the eye that hate me without a cause. For they speak not peace: but they devise deceitful matters against them that are quiet in the land. Yea, they opened their mouth wide against me, and said, Aha, aha, our eye hath seen it. *This thou hast seen, O LORD: keep not silence: O Lord, be not far from me. Stir up thyself, and awake to my judgment, even unto my cause, my God and my Lord. Judge me, O LORD my God, according to thy righteousness; and let them not rejoice over me.* Let them not say in their hearts, Ah, so would we have it: let them not say, We have swallowed him up. Let them be ashamed and brought to confusion together that rejoice at mine hurt: let them be clothed with shame and dishonour that magnify themselves against me. *Let them shout for joy, and be glad, that favour my righteous cause: yea, let them say continually, Let the LORD be magnified, which hath pleasure in the prosperity of his servant. And my tongue shall speak of thy righteousness and of thy praise all the day long.*

Psalm 37:32-34, 39-40 - The wicked watcheth the righteous, and seeketh to slay him. *The LORD will not leave him* [the righteous one] *in his* [the wicked one's] *hand*, nor condemn him when he is judged. *Wait on the LORD, and keep his way, and he shall exalt thee to inherit the land: when the wicked are cut off, thou shalt see it* . . . . *But the salvation of the righteous is of the LORD: he is their strength in the time of trouble. And the LORD shall help them, and deliver them: he shall deliver them from the wicked, and save them, because they trust in him.*

Psalm 38:12-22 - They also that seek after my life lay snares for me: and they that seek my hurt speak mischievous things, and imagine deceits all the day long. But I, as a deaf man, heard not; and I was as a dumb man that openeth not his mouth. Thus I was as a man that heareth not, and in whose mouth are no reproofs.

For in thee, O LORD, do I hope: thou wilt hear, O Lord my God. For I said, Hear me, lest otherwise they should rejoice over me: when my foot slippeth, they magnify themselves against me. For I am ready to halt, and my sorrow is continually before me. *For I will declare mine iniquity; I will be sorry for my sin.* But mine enemies are lively, and they are strong: and they that hate me wrongfully are multiplied. They also that render evil for good are mine adversaries; *because I follow the thing that good is. Forsake me not, O LORD: O my God, be not far from me. Make haste to help me, O Lord my salvation.*

Psalm 40:14-17 - Let them be ashamed and confounded together that seek after my soul to destroy it; let them be driven backward and put to shame that wish me evil. Let them be desolate for a reward of their shame that say unto me, Aha, aha. *Let all those that seek thee rejoice and be glad in thee: let such as love thy salvation say continually, The LORD be magnified. But I am poor and needy; yet the Lord thinketh upon me: thou art my help and my deliverer; make no tarrying, O my God.*

Psalm 42:9-11 - I will say unto God my rock, Why hast thou forgotten me? Why go I mourning because of the oppression of the enemy? As with a sword in my bones, mine enemies reproach me; while they say daily unto me, Where is thy God? Why art thou cast down, O my soul? And why art thou disquieted within me? *Hope thou in God: for I shall yet praise him, who is the health of my countenance, and my God.*

Psalm 43:1-5 - Judge me, O God, and plead my cause against an ungodly nation: O deliver me from the deceitful and unjust man. *For thou art the God of my*

strength: why dost thou cast me off? Why go I mourning because of the oppression of the enemy? *O send out thy light and thy truth: let them lead me; let them bring me unto thy holy hill, and to thy tabernacles. Then will I go unto the altar of God, unto God my exceeding joy: yea, upon the harp will I praise thee, O God my God.* Why art thou cast down, O my soul? And why art thou disquieted within me? *Hope in God: for I shall yet praise him, who is the health of my countenance, and my God.*

Psalm 54:1-7 - *Save me, O God, by thy name, and judge me by thy strength. Hear my prayer, O God; give ear to the words of my mouth.* For strangers are risen up against me, and oppressors seek after my soul: they have not set God before them. Selah. *Behold, God is mine helper*: the Lord is with them that uphold my soul. He shall reward evil unto mine enemies: cut them off in thy truth. *I will freely sacrifice unto thee: I will praise thy name, O LORD; for it is good. For he hath delivered me out of all trouble*: and mine eye hath seen his desire upon mine enemies.

Psalm 55:1-7, 16-18, 22-23 - *Give ear to my prayer, O God; and hide not thyself from my supplication. Attend unto me, and hear me*: I mourn in my complaint, and make a noise; because of the voice of the enemy, because of the oppression of the wicked: for they cast iniquity upon me, and in wrath they hate me. My heart is sore pained within me: and the terrors of death are fallen upon me. Fearfulness and trembling are come upon me, and horror hath overwhelmed me. And I said, Oh that I had wings like a dove! For then would I fly away, and be at rest. Lo, then would I wander far off, and remain in the wilderness. Selah . . . . *As for me, I* *will call upon God; and the LORD shall save me. Evening, and morning, and at noon, will I pray, and cry aloud: and he shall hear my voice. He hath delivered my soul in peace from the battle that was against me*: for there were many with me . . . . *Cast thy burden upon the LORD, and he shall sustain thee: he shall never suffer the righteous to be moved.* But thou, O God, shalt bring them down into the pit of destruction: bloody and deceitful men shall not live out half their days; but I will trust in thee.

Psalm 56:1-4 - *Be merciful unto me, O God*: for man would swallow me up; he fighting daily oppresseth me. Mine enemies would daily swallow me up: for they be many that fight against me, O thou most High. *What time I am afraid, I will trust in thee. In God I will praise his word, in God I have put my trust; I will not fear what flesh can do unto me.*

Psalm 57:1-7 - *Be merciful unto me, O God, be merciful unto me: for my soul trusteth in thee: yea, in the shadow of thy wings will I make my refuge, until these calamities be overpast. I will cry unto God most high; unto God that performeth all things for me. He shall send from heaven, and save me from the reproach of him that would swallow me up.* Selah. *God shall send forth his mercy and his truth.* My soul is among lions: and I lie even among them that are set on fire, even the sons of men, whose teeth are spears and arrows, and their tongue a sharp sword. *Be thou exalted, O God, above the heavens; let thy glory be above all the earth.* They have prepared a net for my steps; my soul is bowed down: they have digged a pit before me, into the midst whereof they are fallen themselves. Selah. *My heart is fixed, O God, my heart is fixed: I will sing and give praise.*

Psalm 59:1-4, 9, 16-17 - *Deliver me from mine enemies, O my God: defend me from them that rise up against me. Deliver me from the workers of iniquity, and save me from bloody men.* For, lo, they lie in wait for my soul: the mighty are gathered against me; not for my transgression, nor for my sin, O LORD. They run and prepare themselves without my fault: *awake to help me, and behold . . . . Because of his strength will I wait upon thee: for God is my defence . . . . But I will sing of thy power; yea, I will sing aloud of thy mercy in the morning: for thou hast been my defence and refuge in the day of my trouble. Unto thee, O my strength, will I sing: for God is my defence, and the God of my mercy.*

Psalm 60:11-12 - *Give us help from trouble*: for vain is the help of man. *Through God we shall do valiantly: for he it is that shall tread down our enemies.*

Psalm 62:5-8 - *My soul, wait thou only upon God; for my expectation is from him. He only is my rock and my salvation: he is my defence; I shall not be moved. In God is my salvation and my glory: the rock of my strength, and my refuge, is in God. Trust in him at all times; ye people, pour out your heart before him: God is a refuge for us.* Selah.

Psalm 64:1-4, 10 - *Hear my voice, O God, in my prayer: preserve my life from fear of the enemy. Hide me from the secret counsel of the wicked; from the insurrection of the workers of iniquity*: who whet their tongue like a sword, and bend their bows to shoot their arrows, even bitter words: that they may shoot in secret at the perfect: suddenly do they shoot at him, and fear not . . . . *The righteous shall be glad in the LORD, and shall trust in him; and all the upright in heart shall glory.*

Psalm 69:1-4, 7-8, 12-18 - *Save me, O God*; for the waters are come in unto my soul. I sink in deep mire, where there is no standing: I am come into deep waters, where the floods overflow me. *I am weary of my crying: my throat is dried: mine eyes fail while I wait for my God.* They that hate me without a cause are more than the hairs of mine head: they that would destroy me, being mine enemies wrongfully, are mighty: then I restored that which I took not away . . . . *Because for thy sake I have borne reproach*; shame hath covered my face. I am become a stranger unto my brethren, and an alien unto my mother's children . . . . They that sit in the gate speak against me; and I was the song of the drunkards. *But as for me, my prayer is unto thee, O LORD, in an acceptable time: O God, in the multitude of thy mercy hear me, in the truth of thy salvation. Deliver me out of the mire, and let me not sink: let me be delivered from them that hate me, and out of the deep waters. Let not the waterflood overflow me, neither let the deep swallow me up, and let not the pit shut her mouth upon me. Hear me, O LORD; for thy lovingkindness is good: turn unto me according to the multitude of thy tender mercies. And hide not thy face from thy servant; for I am in trouble: hear me speedily. Draw nigh unto my soul, and redeem it: deliver me because of mine enemies.*

Psalm 70:1-5 - *Make haste, O God, to deliver me; make haste to help me, O LORD.* Let them be ashamed and confounded that seek after my soul: let them be turned backward, and put to confusion, that desire my hurt. Let them be turned back for a reward of their shame that say, Aha, aha. *Let all those that seek thee rejoice and be glad in thee: and let such as love thy salvation say continually, Let God be magnified. But I am poor and needy: make haste unto me, O God: thou art my help and my deliverer; O LORD, make no tarrying.*

Psalm 71:1-14 - *In thee, O LORD, do I put my trust: let me never be put to confusion. Deliver me in thy righteousness, and cause me to escape: incline thine ear unto me, and save me. Be thou my strong habitation, whereunto I may continually resort: thou hast given commandment to save me; for thou art my rock and my fortress. Deliver me, O my God, out of the hand of the wicked, out of the hand of the unrighteous and cruel man. For thou art my hope, O Lord GOD: thou art my trust from my youth. By thee have I been holden up from the womb: thou art he that took me out of my mother's bowels: my praise shall be continually of thee.* I am as a wonder unto many; *but thou art my strong refuge. Let my mouth be filled with thy praise and with thy honour all the day. Cast me not off in the time of old age; forsake me not when my strength faileth.* For mine enemies speak against me; and they that lay wait for my soul take counsel together, saying, God hath forsaken him: persecute and take him; for there is none to deliver him. *O God, be not far from me: O my God, make haste for my help.* Let them be confounded and consumed that are adversaries to my soul; let them be covered with reproach and dishonour that seek my hurt. *But I will hope continually, and will yet praise thee more and more.*

Psalm 86:14-17 - O God, the proud are risen against me, and the assemblies of violent men have sought after my soul; and have not set thee before them. *But thou, O Lord, art a God full of compassion, and gracious, long-suffering, and plenteous in mercy and truth. O turn unto me, and have mercy upon me; give thy strength unto thy servant, and save the son of thine handmaid. Shew me a token for good; that they which hate me may see it, and be ashamed: because thou, LORD, hast holpen me, and comforted me.*

Psalm 94:14-19 - *For the LORD will not cast off his people, neither will he forsake his inheritance.* But judgment shall return unto righteousness: and all the upright in heart shall follow it. Who will rise up for me against the evildoers? Or who will stand up for me against the workers of iniquity? *Unless the LORD had been my help, my soul had almost dwelt in silence. When I said, My foot slippeth; thy mercy, O LORD, held me up. In the multitude of my thoughts within me thy comforts delight my soul.*

Psalm 102:1-2, 8 - *Hear my prayer, O LORD, and let my cry come unto thee. Hide not thy face from me in the day when I am in trouble; incline thine ear unto me: in the day when I call answer me speedily . . . .* Mine enemies reproach me all the day; and they that are mad against me are sworn against me.

Psalm 109:4, 21-22, 26-27, 30-31 - For my love they are my adversaries: *but I give myself unto prayer . . . . But do thou for me, O GOD the Lord, for thy name's sake: because thy mercy is good, deliver thou me.* For I am poor and needy, and my heart is wounded within me . . . . *Help me, O LORD my God: O save me according to thy mercy: that they may know that this is thy hand; that thou, LORD, hast done it . . . . I will greatly praise the LORD with my mouth; yea, I will praise him among the multitude. For he shall stand at the right hand of the poor, to save him from those that condemn his soul.*

Psalm 118:1, 4-8, 13-14 - *O give thanks unto the LORD; for he is good: because his mercy endureth for ever . . . . Let them now that fear the LORD say, that his mercy endureth for ever. I called upon the LORD in distress: the LORD answered me, and set me in a large* place. *The* LORD *is on my side; I will not fear: what can man do unto me?* *The* LORD *taketh my part with them that help me: therefore shall I see my desire upon them that hate me.* *It is better to trust in the* LORD *than to put confidence in man* . . . . Thou hast thrust sore at me that I might fall: *but the* LORD *helped me.* *The* LORD *is my strength and song, and is become my salvation.*

Psalm 119:22-24, 41-42, 49-52, 61, 67-72, 75-78, 81-88, 92-95, 98, 109-110, 114-117, 121-124, 134, 145-149, 153-157, 161-162 - *Remove from me reproach and contempt; for I have kept thy testimonies.* Princes also did sit and speak against me: *but thy servant did meditate in thy statutes.* *Thy testimonies also are my delight and my counselors* . . . . *Let thy mercies come also unto me, O* LORD, *even thy salvation, according to thy word.* So shall I have wherewith to answer him that reproacheth me: *for I trust in thy word* . . . . *Remember the word unto thy servant, upon which thou hast caused me to hope.* *This is my comfort in my affliction: for thy word hath quickened me.* The proud have had me greatly in derision: *yet have I not declined from thy law.* *I remembered thy judgments of old, O* LORD; *and have comforted myself* . . . . The bands of the wicked have robbed me: *but I have not forgotten thy law* . . . . Before I was afflicted I went astray: *but now have I kept thy word.* *Thou art good, and doest good; teach me thy statutes.* The proud have forged a lie against me: *but I will keep thy precepts with my whole heart.* Their heart is as fat as grease; *but I delight in thy law.* *It is good for me that I have been afflicted; that I might learn thy statutes.* *The law of thy mouth is better unto me than thousands of gold and silver* . . . . *I know, O* LORD, *that thy judgments are right, and that thou in faithfulness*

hast afflicted me. *Let, I pray thee, thy merciful kindness be for my comfort, according to thy word unto thy servant. Let thy tender mercies come unto me, that I may live: for thy law is my delight.* Let the proud be ashamed; for they dealt perversely with me without a cause: ***but I will meditate in thy precepts . . . . My soul fainteth for thy salvation: but I hope in thy word. Mine eyes fail for thy word, saying, When wilt thou comfort me?*** For I am become like a bottle in the smoke; ***yet do I not forget thy statutes.*** How many are the days of thy servant? When wilt thou execute judgment on them that persecute me? The proud have digged pits for me, which are not after thy law. ***All thy commandments are faithful***: they persecute me wrongfully; ***help thou me.*** They had almost consumed me upon earth; ***but I forsook not thy precepts. Quicken me after thy lovingkindness; so shall I keep the testimony of thy mouth . . . . Unless thy law had been my delights, I should then have perished in mine affliction. I will never forget thy precepts: for with them thou hast quickened me. I am thine, save me; for I have sought thy precepts.*** The wicked have waited for me to destroy me: ***but I will consider thy testimonies . . . . Thou through thy commandments hast made me wiser than mine enemies***: for they are ever with me . . . . My soul is continually in my hand: ***yet do I not forget thy law.*** The wicked have laid a snare for me: ***yet I erred not from thy precepts . . . . Thou art my hiding place and my shield: I hope in thy word.*** Depart from me, ye evildoers: ***for I will keep the commandments of my God. Uphold me according unto thy word, that I may live: and let me not be ashamed of my hope. Hold thou me up, and I shall be safe: and I will have respect unto thy statutes continually . . . . I have done judgment and justice: leave me not to mine oppressors. Be surety for thy servant for good: let not the proud***

oppress me. Mine eyes fail for thy salvation, and for the word of thy righteousness. Deal with thy servant according unto thy mercy, and teach me thy statutes . . . . Deliver me from the oppression of man: so will I keep thy precepts . . . . I cried with my whole heart; hear me, O LORD: I will keep thy statutes. I cried unto thee; save me, and I shall keep thy testimonies. I prevented the dawning of the morning, and cried: I hoped in thy word. Mine eyes prevent the night watches, that I might meditate in thy word. Hear my voice according unto thy lovingkindness: O LORD, quicken me according to thy judgment . . . . Consider mine affliction, and deliver me: for I do not forget thy law. Plead my cause, and deliver me: quicken me according to thy word. Salvation is far from the wicked: for they seek not thy statutes. *Great are thy tender mercies, O LORD: quicken me according to thy judgments. Many are my persecutors and mine enemies; yet do I not decline from thy testimonies . . . .* Princes have persecuted me without a cause: *but my heart standeth in awe of thy word. I rejoice at thy word, as one that findeth great spoil.*

Psalm 120:1-2 - *In my distress I cried unto the LORD, and he heard me. Deliver my soul, O LORD, from lying lips, and from a deceitful tongue.*

Psalm 123:1-4 - *Unto thee lift I up mine eyes, O thou that dwellest in the heavens. Behold, as the eyes of servants look unto the hand of their masters, and as the eyes of a maiden unto the hand of her mistress; so our eyes wait upon the LORD our God, until that he have mercy upon us. Have mercy upon us, O LORD, have mercy upon us*: for we are exceedingly filled with contempt. Our soul is exceedingly filled with the scorning of those that are at ease, and with the contempt of the proud.

Psalm 124:1-8 - *If it had not been the LORD who was on our side*, now may Israel say; *if it had not been the LORD who was on our side*, when men rose up against us: then they had swallowed us up quick, when their wrath was kindled against us: then the waters had overwhelmed us, the stream had gone over our soul: then the proud waters had gone over our soul. *Blessed be the LORD, who hath not given us as a prey to their teeth. Our soul is escaped as a bird out of the snare of the fowlers: the snare is broken, and we are escaped. Our help is in the name of the LORD, who made heaven and earth.*

Psalm 138:3, 6-7 - *In the day when I cried thou answeredst me, and strengthenedst me with strength in my soul . . . . Though the LORD be high, yet hath he respect unto the lowly*: but the proud he knoweth afar off. *Though I walk in the midst of trouble, thou wilt revive me*: thou shalt stretch forth thine hand against the wrath of mine enemies, *and thy right hand shall save me.*

Psalm 140:1-8, 12-13 - *Deliver me, O LORD, from the evil man: preserve me from the violent man; which imagine mischiefs in their heart; continually are they gathered together for war.* They have sharpened their tongues like a serpent; adders' poison is under their lips. Selah. *Keep me, O LORD, from the hands of the wicked; preserve me from the violent man; who have purposed to overthrow my goings.* The proud have hid a snare for me, and cords; they have spread a net by the wayside; they have set gins for me. Selah. *I said unto the LORD, Thou art my God: hear the voice of my supplications, O LORD. O GOD the Lord, the strength of my salvation, thou hast covered my head in the day of* *battle. Grant not, O LORD, the desires of the wicked: further not his wicked device; lest they exalt them-selves.* Selah . . . . *I know that the LORD will maintain the cause of the afflicted, and the right of the poor. Surely the righteous shall give thanks unto thy name: the upright shall dwell in thy presence.*

Psalm 141:1, 8-10 - *LORD, I cry unto thee: make haste unto me; give ear unto my voice, when I cry unto thee . . . . But mine eyes are unto thee, O GOD the Lord: in thee is my trust; leave not my soul destitute. Keep me from the snares which they have laid for me, and the gins of the workers of iniquity.* Let the wicked fall into their own nets, *whilst that I withal escape.*

Psalm 142:1-7 - *I cried unto the LORD with my voice; with my voice unto the LORD did I make my supplica-tion. I poured out my complaint before him; I shewed before him my trouble. When my spirit was over-whelmed within me, then thou knewest my path.* In the way wherein I walked have they privily laid a snare for me. I looked on my right hand, and beheld, but there was no man that would know me: refuge failed me; no man cared for my soul. *I cried unto thee, O LORD: I said, Thou art my refuge and my portion in the land of the living. Attend unto my cry; for I am brought very low: deliver me from my persecutors; for they are stronger than I. Bring my soul out of prison, that I may praise thy name: the righteous shall compass me about; for thou shalt deal bountifully with me.*

Psalm 143:1-12 - *Hear my prayer, O LORD, give ear to my supplications: in thy faithfulness answer me, and in thy righteousness.* And enter not into judgment with thy ser-vant: for in thy sight shall no man living be justified. For the enemy hath persecuted my soul; he hath smitten my life down to the ground; he hath made me to dwell in darkness, as those that have been long dead. Therefore is my spirit overwhelmed within me; my heart within me is desolate. *I remember the days of old; I meditate on all thy works; I muse on the work of thy hands. I stretch forth my hands unto thee: my soul thirsteth after thee, as a thirsty land.* Selah. *Hear me speedily, O LORD: my spirit faileth: hide not thy face from me, lest I be like unto them that go down into the pit. Cause me to hear thy lovingkindness in the morning; for in thee do I trust: cause me to know the way wherein I should walk; for I lift up my soul unto thee. Deliver me, O LORD, from mine enemies: I flee unto thee to hide me. Teach me to do thy will; for thou art my God: thy spirit is good; lead me into the land of uprightness. Quicken me, O LORD, for thy name's sake: for thy righteousness' sake bring my soul out of trouble.* And of thy mercy cut off mine enemies, and destroy all them that afflict my soul: for I am thy servant.

Psalm 62:5-8 - *My soul, wait thou only upon God; for my expectation is from him. He only is my rock and my salvation: he is my defence; I shall not be moved. In God is my salvation and my glory: the rock of my strength, and my refuge, is in God. Trust in him at all times; ye people, pour out your heart before him: God is a refuge for us.* Selah.

Isaiah 51:7-8 - *Hearken unto me, ye that know righteousness, the people in whose heart is my law; fear ye not the reproach of men, neither be ye afraid of their revilings.* For the moth shall eat them up like a garment, and the worm shall eat them like wool: but my right-eousness shall be for ever, *and my salvation from generation to generation.*

.

Trust the Lord to Repay Those Who Mistreat You

Leviticus 19:18 - *Thou shalt not avenge, nor bear any grudge against the children of thy people*, but thou shalt love thy neighbour as thyself: I am the LORD.

Proverbs 20:22 - *Say not thou, I will recompense evil*; but wait on the LORD, and he shall save thee.

Proverbs 24:29 - *Say not, I will do so to him as he hath done to me: I will render to the man according to his work.*

Nahum 1:2 - *God is jealous, and the LORD revengeth; the LORD revengeth, and is furious; the LORD will take vengeance on his adversaries, and he reserveth wrath for his enemies.*

Romans 12:19 - *Dearly beloved, avenge not yourselves, but rather give place unto wrath: for it is written, Vengeance is mine; I will repay, saith the Lord.*

1 Corinthians 6:7 - *Now therefore there is utterly a fault among you, because ye go to law one with another. Why do ye not rather take wrong? Why do ye not rather suffer yourselves to be defrauded?*

Deuteronomy 32:35, 39-43 - *To me belongeth vengeance, and recompence; their foot shall slide in due time: for the day of their calamity is at hand, and the things that shall come upon them make haste* . . . . See now that I, even I, am he, and there is no god with me: I kill, and I make alive; I wound, and I heal: *neither is there any that can deliver out of my hand.* For I lift up my hand to heaven, and say, I live for ever. *If I whet my glittering sword, and mine hand take hold on judgment; I will render vengeance to mine enemies, and will reward them that hate me.* I will make mine arrows drunk with blood, and my sword shall devour flesh; and that with the blood of the slain and of the captives, from the beginning of revenges upon the enemy. *Rejoice, O ye nations, with his people: for he will avenge the blood of his servants, and will render vengeance to his adversaries, and will be merciful unto his land, and to his people.*

Psalm 94:1-5, 21-23 - *O LORD God, to whom vengeance belongeth; O God, to whom vengeance belongeth, shew thyself. Lift up thyself, thou judge of the earth: render a reward to the proud.* LORD, how long shall the wicked, how long shall the wicked triumph? How long shall they utter and speak hard things? And all the workers of iniquity boast themselves? *They break in pieces thy people, O LORD, and afflict thine heritage* . . . . *They gather themselves together against the soul of the righteous, and condemn the innocent blood.* But the LORD is my defence; and my God is the rock of my refuge. *And he shall bring upon them their own iniquity, and shall cut them off in their own wickedness; yea, the LORD our God shall cut them off.*

Psalm 3:7 - *Arise, O LORD; save me, O my God: for thou hast smitten all mine enemies upon the cheek bone; thou hast broken the teeth of the ungodly.*

Psalm 5:8-10 - Lead me, O LORD, in thy righteousness because of mine enemies; make thy way straight before my face. For there is no faithfulness in their mouth; their inward part is very wickedness; their throat is an open sepulchre; they flatter with their tongue. *Destroy thou them, O God; let them fall by their own counsels; cast them out in the multitude of their transgressions; for they have rebelled against thee.*

Psalm 7:6, 9-17 - *Arise, O LORD, in thine anger, lift up thyself because of the rage of mine enemies: and awake for me to the judgment that thou hast commanded . . . . Oh let the wickedness of the wicked come to an end*; but establish the just: *for the righteous God trieth the hearts and reins*. My defence is of God, which saveth the upright in heart. God judgeth the righteous, *and God is angry with the wicked every day. If he* [the wicked persecutor] *turn not, he* [the Lord our God] *will whet his sword; he hath bent his bow, and made it ready. He* [the Lord our God] *hath also prepared for him* [for the wicked persecutor] *the instruments of death; he ordaineth his arrows against the persecutors.* Behold, he [the wicked persecutor] travaileth with iniquity, and hath conceived mischief, and brought forth falsehood. *He* [the wicked persecutor] *made a pit, and digged it, and is fallen into the ditch which he made. His mischief shall return upon his own head, and his violent dealing shall come down upon his own pate.* I will praise the LORD according to his righteousness: and will sing praise to the name of the LORD most high.

Psalm 9:3-6, 13-16 - *When mine enemies are turned back, they shall fall and perish at thy presence. For thou hast maintained my right and my cause; thou satest in the throne judging right. Thou hast rebuked the heathen, thou hast destroyed the wicked, thou hast put out their name for ever and ever. O thou enemy, destructtions are come to a perpetual end: and thou hast destroyed cities; their memorial is perished with them* .... Have mercy upon me, O LORD; consider my trouble which I suffer of them that hate me, thou that liftest me up from the gates of death: that I may shew forth all thy praise in the gates of the daughter of Zion: I will rejoice in thy salvation. *The heathen are sunk down in the pit that they made: in the net which they hid is their own foot taken. The LORD is known by the judgment which he executeth: the wicked is snared in the work of his own hands.* Higgaion. Selah.

Psalm 10:1-16 - Why standest thou afar off, O LORD? Why hidest thou thyself in times of trouble? *The wicked in his pride doth persecute the poor: let them be taken in the devices that they have imagined.* For the wicked boasteth of his heart's desire, and blesseth the covetous, whom the LORD abhorreth. The wicked, through the pride of his countenance, will not seek after God: God is not in all his thoughts. His ways are always grievous; thy judgments are far above out of his sight: as for all his enemies, he puffeth at them. He hath said in his heart, I shall not be moved: for I shall never be in adversity. His mouth is full of cursing and deceit and fraud: under his tongue is mischief and vanity. *He sitteth in the lurking places of the villages: in the secret places doth he murder the innocent: his eyes are privily set against the poor. He lieth in wait secretly as a lion in his den: he lieth in wait to catch the poor: he doth* *catch the poor, when he draweth him into his net. He croucheth, and humbleth himself, that the poor may fall by his strong ones. He hath said in his heart, God hath forgotten: he hideth his face; he will never see it.* Arise, O LORD; O God, lift up thine hand: forget not the humble. Wherefore doth the wicked contemn God? *He hath said in his heart, Thou wilt not require it. Thou hast seen it; for thou beholdest mischief and spite, to requite it with thy hand*: the poor committeth himself unto thee; thou art the helper of the fatherless. *Break thou the arm of the wicked and the evil man: seek out his wickedness till thou find none. T he LORD is King for ever and ever: the heathen are perished out of his land.*

Psalm 11:1-7 - In the LORD put I my trust: how say ye to my soul, Flee as a bird to your mountain? *For, lo, the wicked bend their bow, they make ready their arrow upon the string, that they may privily shoot at the upright in heart.* If the foundations be destroyed, what can the righteous do? *The LORD is in his holy temple, the LORD'S throne is in heaven: his eyes behold, his eyelids try, the children of men.* The LORD trieth the righteous: *but the wicked and him that loveth violence his soul hateth. Upon the wicked he shall rain snares, fire and brimstone, and an horrible tempest: this shall be the portion of their cup.* For the righteous LORD loveth righteousness; his countenance doth behold the upright.

Psalm 18:4-8, 13-14, 47 - The sorrows of death compassed me, *and the floods of ungodly men made me afraid*. The sorrows of hell compassed me about: the snares of death prevented me. In my distress I called upon the LORD, and cried unto my God: he heard my voice out of his temple, and my cry came before him, even into his ears. *Then the earth shook and trembled; the foundations also of the hills moved and were shaken, because he was wroth. There went up a smoke out of his nostrils, and fire out of his mouth devoured: coals were kindled by it* . . . . *The* LORD *also thundered in the heavens, and the Highest gave his voice; hail stones and coals of fire. Yea, he sent out his arrows, and scattered them; and he shot out lightnings, and discomfited them* . . . . *It is God that avengeth me*, and subdueth the people under me.

Psalm 27:1-2 - The LORD is my light and my salvation; whom shall I fear? The LORD is the strength of my life; of whom shall I be afraid? *When the wicked, even mine enemies and my foes, came upon me to eat up my flesh, they stumbled and fell.*

Psalm 28:3-5 - Draw me not away with the wicked, and with the workers of iniquity, *which speak peace to their neighbours, but mischief is in their hearts. Give them according to their deeds, and according to the wickedness of their endeavours: give them after the work of their hands; render to them their desert. Because they regard not the works of the* LORD, *nor the operation of his hands, he shall destroy them, and not build them up.*

Psalm 31:17-18, 23 - Let me not be ashamed, O LORD; for I have called upon thee: *let the wicked be ashamed, and let them be silent in the grave. Let the lying lips be put to silence; which speak grievous things proudly and contemptuously against the righteous* . . . . O love the LORD, all ye his saints: for the LORD preserveth the faithful, *and plentifully rewardeth the proud doer.*

Psalm 35:1-8, 26 - *Plead my cause, O LORD, with them that strive with me: fight against them that fight against me. Take hold of shield and buckler, and stand up for mine help. Draw out also the spear, and stop the way against them that persecute me*: say unto my soul, I am thy salvation. *Let them be confounded and put to shame that seek after my soul: let them be turned back and brought to confusion that devise my hurt. Let them be as chaff before the wind: and let the angel of the LORD chase them. Let their way be dark and slippery: and let the angel of the LORD persecute them. For without cause have they hid for me their net in a pit, which without cause they have digged for my soul. Let destruction come upon him at unawares; and let his net that he hath hid catch himself: into that very destruction let him fall . . . . Let them be ashamed and brought to confusion together that rejoice at mine hurt: let them be clothed with shame and dishonour that magnify themselves against me.*

Psalm 36:11-12 - Let not the foot of pride come against me, and let not the hand of the wicked remove me. *There are the workers of iniquity fallen: they are cast down, and shall not be able to rise.*

Psalm 37:12-15 - *The wicked plotteth against the just, and gnasheth upon him with his teeth. The Lord shall laugh at him: for he seeth that his day is coming. The wicked have drawn out the sword, and have bent their bow, to cast down the poor and needy, and to slay such as be of upright conversation. Their sword shall enter into their own heart, and their bows shall be broken.*

Psalm 40:14-15 - *Let them be ashamed and confounded together that seek after my soul to destroy it;*

let them be driven backward and put to shame that wish me evil. Let them be desolate for a reward of their shame that say unto me, Aha, aha.

Psalm 54:4-7 - Behold, God is mine helper: the Lord is with them that uphold my soul. *He shall reward evil unto mine enemies: cut them off in thy truth.* I will freely sacrifice unto thee: I will praise thy name, O LORD; for it is good. For he hath delivered me out of all trouble: *and mine eye hath seen his desire upon mine enemies.*

Psalm 55:9-15, 19-23 - *Destroy, O Lord, and divide their tongues*: for I have seen violence and strife in the city. Day and night they go about it upon the walls thereof: mischief also and sorrow are in the midst of it. Wickedness is in the midst thereof: deceit and guile depart not from her streets. *For it was not an enemy that reproached me; then I could have borne it: neither was it he that hated me that did magnify himself against me; then I would have hid myself from him: but it was thou, a man mine equal, my guide, and mine acquaintance.* We took sweet counsel together, and walked unto the house of God in company. *Let death seize upon them, and let them go down quick into hell: for wickedness is in their dwellings, and among them* .... *God shall hear, and afflict them, even he that abideth of old.* Selah. Because they have no changes, therefore they fear not God. *He hath put forth his hands against such as be at peace with him: he hath broken his covenant. The words of his mouth were smoother than butter, but war was in his heart: his words were softer than oil, yet were they drawn swords.* Cast thy burden upon the LORD, and he shall sustain thee: he shall never suffer the righteous to be moved. *But thou, O God,* *shalt bring them down into the pit of destruction: bloody and deceitful men shall not live out half their days*; but I will trust in thee.

Psalm 56:5-7 - *Every day they wrest my words: all their thoughts are against me for evil. They gather themselves together, they hide themselves, they mark my steps, when they wait for my soul.* Shall they escape by iniquity? *In thine anger cast down the people, O God.*

Psalm 59:5-13 - *Thou therefore, O LORD God of hosts, the God of Israel, awake to visit all the heathen: be not merciful to any wicked transgressors.* Selah. They return at evening: they make a noise like a dog, and go round about the city. Behold, they belch out with their mouth: *swords are in their lips*: for who, say they, doth hear? *But thou, O LORD, shalt laugh at them; thou shalt have all the heathen in derision.* Because of his strength will I wait upon thee: for God is my defence. The God of my mercy shall prevent me: *God shall let me see my desire upon mine enemies.* Slay them not, lest my people forget: *scatter them by thy power; and bring them down, O Lord our shield. For the sin of their mouth and the words of their lips let them even be taken in their pride: and for cursing and lying which they speak. Consume them in wrath, consume them, that they may not be: and let them know that God ruleth in Jacob unto the ends of the earth.* Selah.

Psalm 60:12 - Through God we shall do valiantly: *for he it is that shall tread down our enemies*.

Psalm 62:3 - How long will ye imagine mischief against a man? *Ye shall be slain all of you: as a bowing wall shall ye be, and as a tottering fence.*

Psalm 64:5-9 - They encourage themselves in an evil matter: they commune of laying snares privily; they say, Who shall see them? They search out iniquities; they accomplish a diligent search: both the inward thought of every one of them, and the heart, is deep. *But God shall shoot at them with an arrow; suddenly shall they be wounded. So they shall make their own tongue to fall upon themselves: all that see them shall flee away. And all men shall fear, and shall declare the work of God; for they shall wisely consider of his doing.*

Psalm 69:19-28 - Thou hast known my reproach, and my shame, and my dishonour: mine adversaries are all before thee. Reproach hath broken my heart; and I am full of heaviness: and I looked for some to take pity, but there was none; and for comforters, but I found none. They gave me also gall for my meat; and in my thirst they gave me vinegar to drink. *Let their table become a snare before them: and that which should have been for their welfare, let it become a trap. Let their eyes be darkened, that they see not; and make their loins continually to shake. Pour out thine indignation upon them, and let thy wrathful anger take hold of them. Let their habitation be desolate; and let none dwell in their tents. For they persecute him whom thou hast smitten; and they talk to the grief of those whom thou hast wounded. Add iniquity unto their iniquity: and let them not come into thy righteousness. Let them be blotted out of the book of the living, and not be written with the righteous.*

Psalm 70:1-3 - *Make haste, O God, to deliver me; make haste to help me, O LORD. Let them be ashamed and confounded that seek after my soul: let them be turned backward, and put to confusion, that desire my hurt.*

Let them be turned back for a reward of their shame that say, Aha, aha.

Psalm 71:10-13, 24 - *For mine enemies speak against me; and they that lay wait for my soul take counsel together, saying, God hath forsaken him: persecute and take him; for there is none to deliver him.* O God, be not far from me: O my God, make haste for my help. *Let them be confounded and consumed that are adversaries to my soul; let them be covered with reproach and dishonour that seek my hurt* .... My tongue also shall talk of thy righteousness all the day long: *for they are confounded, for they are brought unto shame, that seek my hurt.*

Psalm 109:1-20, 28-29 - *Hold not thy peace, O God of my praise*; for the mouth of the wicked and the mouth of the deceitful are opened against me: they have spoken against me with a lying tongue. They compassed me about also with words of hatred; and fought against me without a cause. For my love they are my adversaries: but I give myself unto prayer. And they have rewarded me evil for good, and hatred for my love. *Set thou a wicked man over him: and let Satan stand at his right hand. When he shall be judged, let him be condemned: and let his prayer become sin. Let his days be few; and let another take his office. Let his children be fatherless, and his wife a widow. Let his children be continually vagabonds, and beg: let them seek their bread also out of their desolate places. Let the extortioner catch all that he hath; and let the strangers spoil his labour. Let there be none to extend mercy unto him: neither let there be any to favour his fatherless children. Let his posterity be cut off; and in the generation following let their name be blotted out. Let the* *iniquity of his fathers be remembered with the LORD; and let not the sin of his mother be blotted out. Let them be before the LORD continually, that he may cut off the memory of them from the earth.* Because that he remembered not to shew mercy, but persecuted the poor and needy man, that he might even slay the broken in heart. *As he loved cursing, so let it come unto him: as he delighted not in blessing, so let it be far from him. As he clothed himself with cursing like as with his garment, so let it come into his bowels like water, and like oil into his bones. Let it be unto him as the garment which covereth him, and for a girdle wherewith he is girded continually. Let this be the reward of mine adversaries from the LORD, and of them that speak evil against my soul* . . . . Let them curse, but bless thou: *when they arise, let them be ashamed*; but let thy servant rejoice. *Let mine adversaries be clothed with shame, and let them cover themselves with their own confusion, as with a mantle.*

Psalm 138:7 - Though I walk in the midst of trouble, thou wilt revive me: *thou shalt stretch forth thine hand against the wrath of mine enemies*, and thy right hand shall save me.

Psalm 140:9-11 - *As for the head of those that compass me about, let the mischief of their own lips cover them. Let burning coals fall upon them: let them be cast into the fire; into deep pits, that they rise not up again. Let not an evil speaker be established in the earth: evil shall hunt the violent man to overthrow him.*

Psalm 143:12 - *And of thy mercy cut off mine enemies, and destroy all them that afflict my soul: for I am thy servant.*

Isaiah 51:7-8 - Hearken unto me, ye that know right-eousness, the people in whose heart is my law; *fear ye not the reproach of men, neither be ye afraid of their revilings. For the moth shall eat them up like a gar-ment, and the worm shall eat them like wool*: but my righteousness shall be for ever, and my salvation from generation to generation.

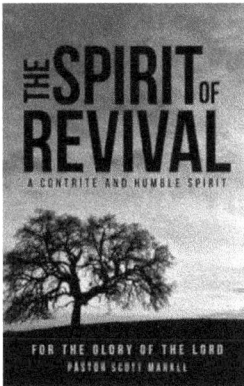